C000156757

Anthology No.3

Brampton Poets 2021

Copyright © 2021 Brampton Poetry Group

The right of the Brampton Poetry Group to be identified as the Author of the Work has been asserted by them in accordance Copyrights, Designs and Patents Act 1988.
The Copyright for each poem resides with its author. All images are the property of the authors or illustrators or freely available in the public domain.

First Published in 2021 by Brampton Poets 2021

Apart from any use permitted under UK copyright law, this publication may only be reproduced, stored in a retrieval system, or transmitted, in any form, or by any means, with prior permission in writing of the publisher or, in the case of reprographic production, in accordance with the terms of licenses issued by the Copyright Licensing Agency.

All characters and events in this publication, other than those clearly in the public domain, are fictitious and any resemblance to real persons, living or dead, is purely coincidental.

Note:

This collection of poetry was begun during the 2021 COVID-19 lockdown period. Our thoughts, of course, are with all those near and far that continue to be affected by this awful pandemic. Any profits, beyond publication costs and the associated overheads of the Brampton Poetry Group will again be gifted to an NHS related Charity within our area – with our thanks and in awe of their contribution!

Brampton Poets 2021

CONTENTS

Ena Hutchinson 62

Ruth Kershaw 68

Acknowledgements

Our heartfelt thanks are due to the *Cottage Coffee community* for the financial assistance that made the publication of the first anthology possible. We have now been inspired to attempt both a second and a third!

Preface

Brampton Poets is a name assumed by a group of people who meet monthly in the Community Centre in Brampton. The group was born out of a Poetry Breakfast event in the Theatre by the Lake in Keswick in 2016, under the umbrella of Words by the Water, at which people were invited to gather for breakfast and to read poetry: their own or that of others.

Ena and Gilbert Hutchinson, Brampton residents, brought the concept back to Brampton, contacted a number of acquaintances whom they knew to be interested in poetry and suggested adopting the same format on a monthly basis.

When circumstances again allow the group aims to continue to meet at 10 a.m. on the first Thursday of every month, enjoy a croissant, a cup of tea and a chat for half an hour, before reading and discussing poetry for a period of 45 minutes to an hour.

The theme of this third anthology 'journeying' was prompted by the experiences, both individual and shared, that we have all been through over the last 12months or so.

The Poets

David Bamford

David Bamford came to live in Lanercost in 2010 after having worked in education in South America for 22 out of the previous 25 years. He returned to UK to retire, but soon found himself working part time at Austin Friars School in Carlisle, teaching Spanish, until they ran out of hours for him. Shortly after retiring for the second time, he was offered a few hours teaching French at Hayton C. of E. Primary School, which he loves.

David has had a love of poetry for as long as he can remember and numbers poets among his forebears. He is also a Reader in the Church of England, an active participant in theatrical activities and an inveterate writer of letters to the Cumberland News.

He sees poetry as a form of written expression that captures a moment of inspiration and fixes it as a kind of epiphany (and he hopes that doesn't sound too pompous!).

David Hurd

David Hurd was born in 1940, went to Irthing Valley School but left at 14 to join the Army Apprentice School in Harrogate, and served 18 years in Survey, Royal Engineers until made redundant.

He served 5½ years in Singapore, the rest in the south of England. After the army he spent 4 years in Edinburgh at Bartholomew's, creating maps and atlases.

David then moved to Carlisle to Metal Box for 3 years, then to a small printing works in Brampton for 10 years until made redundant. He then went to Carlisle College of Art for 4yrs.

His interests vary through metal sculpture, wood carving, stained glass work and fibreglass work, and finally poetry which he has written most of his life. He wrote quite a bit whilst in Singapore.

The theme for this volume is 'the journey and travel', to Singapore, commuted and courted, wed and buried his wife Eva. The latest episodes in his life contain comments on Coronovirus.

Ena R. E. Hutchinson

Ena was born in Harrogate Golf Club in 1936 where her parents were living as Steward and Stewardess. During World War II Ena, a younger brother and two younger cousins were all brought up together as one family, with grandparents and aunt, while the fathers were serving abroad.

On leaving secondary school, Ena attended Harrogate Technical College for Catering. Leaving there at 16, she undertook a two-year managerial course in London with J Lyons & Co. before returning to Yorkshire to be with her grandmother after her grandfather's death. Ena married her first husband in 1958 and had two sons and, later, six grandchildren.

With a career as a self-employed caterer, Ena moved North to Preston in 1964 and then into the Borders. In the early 1980s, Ena ran the Cathedral Buttery - as it was in those days.

Ena met Gilbert in 1985. They were married in 1986 and moved to Brampton in 2002. They shared a love of walking, nature, books and music, and Ena came to appreciate poetry. Following trips to 'The Theatre by the Lake' in early 2016, the idea of a Brampton Poets Group was formed and, following encouragement, launched.

Ruth Kershaw

Ruth has lived in Brampton for 50 years. She was born in Rochdale, but, due to her father's promotions on the railway, found herself in Halifax by the time she was 10. Here she stayed until she had gained School Certificate. Now at the northern end of the chain, Ruth thinks of herself as a Pennine woman and revels in their wildness. She has walked the Pennine Way.

A long period of bedrest (age 6 rheumatic fever) gave time to indulge in Arthur Mee's encyclopedia, the Poetry and Natural History sections laying foundation for lifelong interests.

She is indebted to her English teacher for encouraging her to write essays but did not venture into poetry until 2013 when she enjoyed a Poetry Course at Stones Barn, Roweltown, North Cumbria, led by Ian Duhig. Immediately "hooked" she has attended 2 more of the same.

A retired Methodist Minister, she finds poems easier than sermons.

John S Langley

John Langley was born and raised in the North East of England and has two brothers, three sons and only one wife.

After qualifying as a Chemical Engineer he was lucky enough to work around the world on various projects before moving into Consultancy and finally becoming his own Company.

He has enjoyed writing creatively all his life, a trait that was not always appreciated whilst at school, but the disciplines of Technical Report writing put something of a dampener on this for about 30 years.

Now settled back in the North he has time to write with freedom and experimentation and has even built up enough courage to admit to being an Author and a Poet. In 2020 he completed and was awarded an MA(poetry) by the Open University.

Doreen Moscrop

Doreen was born and educated in Brampton and has now returned here to live. Having had a varied career in accountancy, shepherding, and office management, she has always maintained a great affection for the countryside and the Lake District. She began walking seriously in Lakeland in 1994, completing the Lake rounds and then the highest mountains, in preparation for her charity walks of Snowdon and Ben Nevis. Her final challenge was to visit all 214 named tarns in the National Park. These pursuits were her inspiration for returning to her painting and poetry composing pastimes.

Jean Taylor

Jean lived in Hethersgill Cumbria for 25 years and then in Brampton for the past 4 years. She was born in Liverpool in 1932 and joined Martins Bank (which later became Barclays Bank) in 1948 at the age of 16 – the youngest person to join. In 1954 Jean joined the Wrens and worked in The Admiralty Building in London. Having left the Wrens in 1956 to get married Jean had 4 children and worked alongside her husband running their own dairy business in Liverpool until they both retired aged 61 and moved to Cumbria.

Jean wrote her first poem when she was 87 and it was included in last year's Anthology. The two poems in this Anthology were written when she was 88.

Stuart Turner

Stuart Turner was born on 7th May 1942 in Newcastle and spent his childhood in Consett, a steel town in County Durham (the Steel Works closed in 1980). He belongs very much to the Christian family and the upholding of Christian traditions. He attended Annfield Plain Secondary Modern School and was introduced to Literature, in particular, by his Headmaster, who was a brilliant man with the iconic name of W.E.Gladstone.

He started writing poetry in1962 after he joined the Royal Air Force and concentrated more specifically on this after the millennium in 2000 when he had more time after raising a family. He has engaged in both verse and prose, and his writing usually focuses on a mixture of nature and human interaction.

The Poems

David Bamford

Limbo

The word that provides a theme for this collection of musings is prompted by the fact that we sold the house in which we had lived for ten years and, in order to give ourselves time to decide where to look for more permanent, lodgings, went into rented accommodation.

A state between two other states,
that is between what was
and what may be.
Neither one thing nor the other;
between stability
and what is yet unknown,
unproved, unsavoured.

A rocking, uncertain instability,
an oarless boat upon the current.
No rudder with which to steer a course.
We are dependent on the swirls,
the twists and turn of current.

A little to the north,
I see the river Eden
flowing eastwards.
Wait. That can't be right.
It flows through Carlisle, to the west.

Ah yes, meandering, not straight.
The river's in a limbo too,
pausing, taking stock
before she flows
to where she is supposed to go.

Crossing

*While taking the ferry from Belfast to Cairnryan
one afternoon in January 2020, I pondered on the
simplicity of travel between Northern Ireland and
England and how post-Brexit border arrangements
might affect this.*

Leaving the sun behind
in the pink-tinged west,
we glide through Belfast Lough
towards the Irish Sea,
past Carrickfergus on the left,
or should I say to Port?
To Starboard, Holywood
- one 'l', not two -,
where we walked yesterday,
Bangor, Helen's Bay.

Slowly and majestically, the hum
and imperceptible throb
of mighty engines
make us forge a gentle furrow
towards the dusk-gathering east,
where the Mull of Galloway
extends its arm, beckons,
draws us like a magnet
to Scotland's western shore.

Will there be a border here,
Where none exists?
An expanse of water,
blue-grey-green,
flat, shifting, unperturbed
and not disturbed
except by a ferry that inscribes a line
into its surface,
from west to east,
not north to south.
It doesn't last. It's gone.

The sea-wash covers our wake
and churning foam
returns once more to water,
covers and obliterates the ferry's course
and leaves no scar to mark our passage.

This is travel
within a kingdom.
No restriction, no control.
Freedom of passage
across no border
and within one realm.

Quiet desperation

During the lockdown, what was there to do but wait
while time passed? Horizons shrank to the walls
within which we lived or to a radius of a mile
around us. It wasn't much fun, really.

Passing days.
A lockdown locks us up.
The sun travels the sky from east to south to west.
Birds flap lazy flights from tree to tree.
We sit, we watch, we wait,
for what?
For the ache of loneliness to pass,
to talk to people face to face,
with no more Zoom, Whatsapp, Skype,
Facebook, FaceTime or telephone.
But real contact, eye contact,
a smile, a handshake or a hug,
the marks of friendship, kinship
that we're in danger of forgetting.

What day's today?
The one after yesterday,
And what was yesterday?
I no longer know
nor care
very much.
It doesn't make much difference.
Will things change tomorrow?
What day's tomorrow,
but the one after today?

The days are much the same.
We wake up,
have breakfast,
wash up, then wait for lunch,
linger through the afternoon
and then prepare an evening meal,
maybe,
or think about it.

Meanwhile, here we are,
locked down, locked up,
locked in.
In quarantine,
while life goes on outside.

Or does it?

Legacy

*During the Coronavirus lockdown, life assumed a limbic
quality. We had no idea how long it was going to last,
whether we would get through it, - many did not - nor what
it would be like when it was over.*

When this is over
and life returns to 'normal,'
where will we find ourselves?
Will we move on?
Lick wounds
and shrug our shoulders?
Consider it a blip
upon a landscape of experience?
Say 'that's life,'
shake off the dust
and be as we once were?
Jump back into our cars,
belch fumes into the atmosphere,
an atmosphere that had grown cleaner,
throw rubbish onto verges
and on surfaces of highways?
Gather once again
as the noisy rabble that we were before?

Or will we recognise the sacrifice
of those who put their lives upon the line
and who,
ignoring risk and danger to themselves,
worked round the clock
to keep *us* safe?

To those who strove,
we owe our gratitude,
in our responsibility
to make of their example
our watchword,
principle and lodestar,
to play our part in keeping
this world safe
for those with whom we share it
and to whom we pass it on.

Waiting Room

During the course of May 2020, when the weather turned severe, we went down to Chester, where part of our family lives. We went by train; we usually do, as it's easier. There were considerable disruptions and, on the way back, we had a long wait on Warrington Bank Quay station. This is not the most exciting railway station in the country, but nothing need stop the use of our senses.

Red and shades of grey,
impassive passengers
waiting in a void
of suspended time.
Trains delayed, timetables disrupted,
the aftermath of Storm Ciara,
'the storm of the century.'
Inflated claim
with eighty years to go.

Dismantled climate,
all upside down,
torrential rain
and biting wind
upsetting our dependence
on time and space.
Timetables, schedules,
set in stone,
fixed, immutable,
except when weather cries 'havoc!'
and lets slip the dogs of chaos,
while we, all passive victims

await our fate,
rustle pages of our newspapers,
attend to tinkling phones
and anxious questions:
'Where are you?'
'When will you be home?'
'Did you forget the meeting?'
Or instructions, once essential,
now of no importance:
'Don't forget the milk.'
'Wait outside the station.'
Fine, but when will I arrive.
A victim of delay?

There's nothing we can do,
but wait,
inactive pawns
among the red
and shades of grey.

The tunnel

*13th April 2020. The situation in which we are living
has been referred to as a tunnel, with or without
light at the end of it. This is, perhaps, an obvious
metaphor.*

I'm going through a tunnel
on my own,
observing social distance,
because I'm of an age
when I'm at risk.
I have a friend, inclined to say,
with frequency,
'mortality's a hundred per cent.'
We are all aware of this,
and no light
does it help to cast
upon the tunnel's walls,
nor upon its end.

I smell the damp,
the fear,
the helplessness.
I hear the drip
of drops of water as they fall,
counting passing time,
I, too, count passing time,
as I move on.
One foot and then the other.
I say a prayer,
'Lord, help me through.'

Vicissitudes

I love the word, although I don't care greatly for what it describes. Nevertheless, I suppose we are all subjected to them at one time or another. The word seemed to lend itself to an acrostic.

Various ups and downs of life
Invading our complacency
Cut through the flimsy fabric of our confidence
Interrupting rhythms to which we're used
Severing connections and disrupting any
Semblance of cohesion
In patterns that habit has established
Turn upside down the rituals
Upon which we float our fragile raft
Damaging the cords that bind its planks together
Exerting tension-testing tolerance
Severing or cementing our resolve

A moving experience

On Monday 24th August 2020, we moved house. We had been at our previous address for ten years. We had had the house on the market because it and the garden had become too big for us and the management of both had begun to exceed our capacity. We had more or less resigned ourselves to staying there for some time to come, when suddenly, during lockdown, we received an offer that was too good to ignore.

A week ago, last Monday,
we moved,
cleared out ten years of settlement.
What to take and what to leave behind
and what to jettison?
These were the questions that gave us pause.

We have not gone far,
six miles, more or less,
into rented quarters;
the twelfth part of a house, to be precise.
Holme Eden Hall, in nearby Warwick Bridge.

An envelope arrived, addressed to us
at Holme End (sic) Hall.
Was this a portent?
Was this new 'Holme' to be an end,
our final earthly resting place?
I rather hope not.

We still consider, contemplate
a place that is our own,
that we call 'home'
and where we place our mark,
put pictures on the walls
and spread our 'stuff,'
create an album of our life
whose pages future generations
will still want to turn.

We'd like to welcome them
to somewhere that is ours,
contains belongings that
one day they may inherit.
But who can know
whether this may indeed be so?

Thinking about moving

Following our move in August, we set about looking for
somewhere to buy that would see us out until we were
no longer able to fend for ourselves. That's not so
easy. The older one gets, the greater the number of
demands one has and the less one feels disposed to
make do and adapt.

We're looking for a house
that ticks ten boxes.
More downstairs than up,
for stairs get difficult
as we get older.
A downstairs bedroom would be a plus
with, of course, an *en-suite*
bathroom, shower or wet room.
Open plan's preferred,
though not the downstairs loo, of course.
That must have a door
that locks,
and maybe an alarm cord,
just in case.
In case of what?
Well, just in case, you know.

What about a garden?
Somewhere to sit,
to have a cup of coffee
and a chat,
watch the birds
and see the world go by.

Just a little space.
A flower bed or two.
And a shed?
What for?
Well, for your tools.
What tools?
I gave them all away,
except the trowel and little fork,
ah, the strimmer and the watering can
as well.
The pressure washer too, now I come to think,
The toolbox also and its contents
and sundry screws and nails
and shelving;
all those metal units
I took apart and stacked away.

Then there's the folding chairs,
The fire pit and barbecue,
bags of compost, fertiliser,
propagators, pea sticks, bean poles and the like.
All stowed and needing space.

I think we'll just stay put.

Leaving self

*During the last week of September 2020, I set off
with a friend to walk the Whithorn Way, from St
Mungo's Cathedral, in Glasgow, to Whithorn in
South Galloway. This is one of a number of pilgrim
routes in Scotland. We did this in lieu of the Camino
de Santiago through northern Spain, which we had
planned to do, but from which we were prevented
by Covid-induced travel restrictions. Pilgrimage is
an act of self-denial, reduction to the minimum,
getting back to the basic essence of life.*

Leaving self.
No rule, no status,
all functions stripped away.
A lightened load.
Pared to the bone.

A pack contains the need;
a change of clothes,
a sleeping bag,
a minimum of food
for sustenance and energy,
and water, a little and no more,
and dressings for the feet,
for they must carry me
and what I carry.

Walking on,
a destination in my head.
Is it the destination
or the journey that's important?
Time will tell.

Pilgrim-age

*A pilgrimage is a step, really many steps, into the
unknown. A number of such steps, for example, to
Jerusalem, to Mecca, to Santiago de Compostela,
are undertaken with a particular destination in
view. If not a destination, at least a purpose. For
some, it is the destination that is the motivation, for
others, it may be the challenge, the search for some
internal quality. Whatever the case, a pilgrimage is
a form of quest, it requires commitment and
prompts reflection.*

One foot in front of the other,
then the other before the first.
So onward, southward.
We leave the town of Ayr,
golf courses, beaches,
houses built of stone,
to Alloway, the Brig o' Doon
and on.

The feet and walking poles
measure out the miles.
The sky, above, deep blue,
the landscape green on green
and other greens.

Meadows, fields and woods
stitch patchwork on the hills.
Timeless terrain,
yet little sign
of saints who once walked here.

Now cars and tractors,
vans and lorries
are the needles that sew the seams
between the patches
of the fabric on the ground.

We walk, we tread the path.
No hairshirt, pilgrim staff
or begging bowl,
no alms, no caves
in which to lay our head,
no barns in which to crawl
for shelter.
Our nights are spent in comfort,
and yet our feet
do penance on the surface of the road
as we walk on,
for we are bound
for Isle of Whithorn.

Barrhill to New Luce

This was the longest walk of the pilgrimage: 14 miles up onto and over the south Ayrshire moorland and down into the woods of Galloway. Damp mist gave way to high cloud and brilliant blue sky to reveal a wide landscape populated by slowly turning wind turbines. Majestic. A long walk. I reached the end just before it started to rain. I felt blessed.

Across an Ayrshire moorland,
a large expanse of rolling hills.
The road rises, gently, slowly;
the feet and poles measure tread.

Pinewoods felled, reforested.
Wind turbines raise their soaring shafts;
their trefoil tops rotate in measured time.
Don Quixote's giants,
but slender, graceful,
burnished by the autumn sun.

They turn,
I walk.
I walk,
they turn.
They stand,
I move
onward towards the goal,
today.

David Hurd

What! and That!

As soon as I realised that Eva was for life I bought myself a Triumph 250cc scooter, she already had one. Mine was a bit underpowered to convey me from Newbury up to Carlisle, but it was the best to be had. When I was posted to Singapore I left it in the camp.

As I speed away on this southbound train,
This parting comes as a doleful pain,
To weep a while I can't refrain, both
Pain and hurt I can't explain,
Mine eyes are moist, must be the smoke,
I long thy cascade hair to stroke,
What pangs in me thou hast awoke,
Forgive me, I'm a simple bloke.
When first we wandered through the wood,
I thought, perhaps, well maybe, could,
A better find I never would,
Since then I've sort of understood.

When second round our scooters take,
A blustered trip circumference lake,
A blasted cable had to break
And patience a hammering did take,

Penrith we did return our lot,
Despite the cold we all felt hot,
Called for a large full coffee pot,
My fags remained when we did not.
First met we in the theatre club,
Alone yet with a bustling hub,
Since then received we quite a snub,
"Remember where we are we should"
Again in Pirates of Penzance,
And later in their thank-you dance,
A waltz took both within a trance,
And welded firm our first romance.

The table turn to play record
I home did take with one accord,
Nat, and Earl, mutual adored
Hours pleasant, in my memory stored,
Again the theatre Rudigore
And Tosca to our culture store,
Never either seen before,
Remember them for ever more.
Shortly my return I ring
And hope more wonder both will sing,
Before eventual parting bring
The venom of its parting sting.
With you again my heart rejoice
List not to conscience quiet voice,
You are my one, my own, my choice,
With you I'm not the least nervous.

Love is the strongest thing
The oldest and the greatest thing,
I hear the birds, which gently sing,
Messages from you they bring,
Your question "Penny for your thoughts?"
A fortune brass could not be bought,
Corral the pleasures that they brought,
I'd sell nor part with part for naught,
April fourteenth I start my leave,
So short a time I can't believe,
Yet distance, time, absence decreed,
Again with you my arms receive.
Twenty-nine again depart,
Till then we'll live, ruled by the heart,
Correspond once more must start,
G.P.O. play a vital part.
I'll close this ditty, my own dear Eva
With love unbound sincere forever,
This my vow I'll try, endeavour,
Cooling, waning, failing never.

October 1962

I invited Eva and my brother Richard down to
Haslemere to see what the camp and town were like and
also to see what accommodation we were likely to get.

Once more I resort to the verse, I hope it's not the last,
Although maybe it will be worse than others in the past,
To thank you most my love sincere I'll try with this to do,
My talents limited I fear I'll try my best for you,
My thanks to you for coming down to stay with Mrs Saul,
With Richard in your future town, I hope you had a ball,

I'm grateful that you had a car, the chauffeur Dick was Inc',
It's meant that we could travel far, that line leaves much to think.
The night we spent engrossed in talk, our future in the army,
We didn't even take a walk; my Mam would think us balmy,
Better things we had to do like locked in close embrace,
For minutes precious, but so few, in shaded quiet place.

Talking not of Eartha Kitt which Guildford did afford,
I'm sure my love we did our bit to form our own record.
The day we spent in Bognor Regis, the tang of fresh sea air,
Again I humbly pledge allegiance to my love I'll always swear,
A special thank-you for the dance though Dick had much to drink
Your brief stay truly did enhance though worried I did think.

I fear you had so far to go whilst I retire to bed,
My anxious fears unwelcomed grow go buzzing round my head,
I fear maybe your route you miss, pursue and journey o'er the way
Thank God, my heart rejoice, Dick's telegram arrive,
He must have heard my anxious voice, thank goodness you can d

I'm sorry if your bed was hard, least, all accommodate,
Mr Saul, he was a card, a prospect distance fate,
Prospects future aren't too grim a house for us to find,
I'll have a word with other Jim, perhaps he will be kind,
We anxious wait for coming Jan when wedded true we'll be
I'll home at Christmas if I can, if they will let me free,
Until that time my love, my dear, to write I'll have to try,
And meet you in the plains above, whilst sleeping both we lie.

David Hurd Wed Eva Hepple 16 Jan 63

Click   23/12/63

*With all the pop music and carols blaring out
I thought about relating childbirth to musical
instruments and the rest of life as applied to
music and rhythm.*

Gently removed from its membrane sleeve,
And placed upon the table round,
Dust and fragments must relieve,
Or they will mar its perfect sound.
As records go it's just the thing
A solace here the world could find.
A life of pleasure to all must bring,
That's if you treat it good and kind.

Adjust the speed most carefully,
For is not once around a year?
The speakers too, the best must be,
It must not go too fast I fear.
The first sound that you hear is shrill,
Which fades to let you hear the cry.
Born the infant small and still,
Relief and pleasure mum will sigh,

From here of course the tune must flow,
With breath of life and rhythm blow,
Which sighs a lilting lullaby,
The song of life, provokes a cry,
Until the tune does stronger grow,
The flute, replace the piccolo,
The lullaby is soft and firm,
Until the child to crawl, does learn.

Faster now and quick the beat
With bars that echo tapping feet,
Up and down the scale they run
The soloist has lots of fun.
But always in the background near,
The parent note piano hear,
Unaccompanied on the drum,
You soon will hear the school bell rung.

Conducted on this merry dance,
As now the trumpet takes its chance,
The French horn sings out, loud and clear,
As school days end, too soon I fear,
So soon the melody enhance,
For has the record found romance?
Now the baton dance and weave,
Away from us he has to leave.

The trombone blows a hollow note,
But we, as parents, must not dote,
We will join in, and jolly be,
Find in E.P. what L.P. see,
The organ grind, and grate, and blast,
As slow, together, they move past,
Progressing onwards from our song,
To make their own tune just as long.
Our melody is fading now,
Musicians each in turn, must bow,
To exit left, or exit right,
Till all sounds fade and leaves the night,
----st, ---st, --st, -st, click.

November, Sunday night, Singapore. 1963

*Just arrived in Singapore after about 24 hrs
travelling, I'm totally jiggered, but feel obliged to
write to let you know I'm OK I miss you already
night night.*

Jazz and fags
Unpacked bags,
Sweaty and hot
Cholera shot,
T.A.T.B.
Fly oversea,
And overland,
Ain't it grand.
Girl or boy?
Heaven joy,
Both prepare
Love and care,
Squeaky toy
Little boy,
Golden curl
Little girl.
Half past ten
Off agen,
Carry on
Spelling wrong,
Never mind
Rhythm find,

Beatles blare,
I don't care
Sand and dust
Depart we must,
Leave behind
Most unkind,
Trouble strife
Half my life.
Mum and Dad
Proud and glad,
One of three?
Well maybe
Say no more
No to four
Cha-wallah
They holler,
Coffee black
I'll be back,
Cheese roll
Fill a hole.
Half the world
Paper hurled

Try to write
Half the night.
Lick and stick
Pen or bic,
Subject change,
Varied range.
Pair the word
Most absurd,
It amuse,
Express views,
Opinion
Carry on.
Well love
As above,
I must go
Cheerio,
I'll say
For the day,
I'll write
Good night.

Posted Dec 3rd 1963

When you are come to me at last,
And those purgatory months are past,
We'll settle down and start our home
Though miles away across the foam,
Where people, places, strange anew,
In contrast to the ones we knew.
With yellows, whites, and tans and blacks,
Who live in kampongs leafy shacks,
Who cook their broth and rice on fires,
And worship in pagoda spires.

Wear Samphoo, Sarong, Cheongsam neat,
And strut on wooden hobbled feet.
They labour long though not too fast,
Beneath the sun's incessant blast.
Self governed now these people hold
To never more the white-man's fold.
They're proud, these people of the east,
To prove their worth they never cease.
Though pleased enough to work and serve,
Equal standing they deserve.
Never treat as dirt, contempt,
For course enough to have relent.
They build, progress with leap and bound
This can be felt by all around.

The white is still as welcome here,
Children to they do hold dear,
I hope my dear you will enjoy,
With baby be it girl or boy,
Strong in will and limb to grow,
But not as yet to see the snow.
A letter did I say to write,
I've been tapping this thing half the night.

So far I've not a house to rent
But neither all my money spent.
Oh please my darling don't be long.
I want to hear that infant song,
At first I'm sure a blessing be
You're sure my love you still want me?
Well my love its time for bed,
I hope that what I said, I said.
Although I end on octave grave
I give you all the love from Dave.

For Steven's Birthday Dec 23rd 1963

Stuck in Singapore with Eva here in Brampton having the baby ? What was I supposed to do? I do remember being in town with John Heggy crossing Orchard road when I felt a tremendous surge in my stomach I just collapsed in the middle of the road, John picked me up carried me into the Magnolia milk bar, I said

"Steven's born"

That mystic place above the cloud through layers of strata seven,
Where winds and breezes can be found, that trumpet blow for Steven
Where anthems raise and voices sing their cry o'er all the earth,
That tiny mite to us doth bring, the magic joy of birth.

Though frail and feeble, meek and mild, this tot of tender age,
We thank you for this little child, life's story's future page,
So soon my love will come the day, when life and limb grow strong,
When laughter rich and childish gay, rejoice in youth and song.

When older still and wiser yet gain strength in mind and will,
Schooled more in life, more knowledge get, his proper place to fill.
In future years we will look back, recall tomorrows dawn,
The pleasures of this life we pack, since days when we were born.

I hope and pray with all my heart, as parents undertake,
God grant us power to do our part, success our best to make,
I want no one who's brave and bold, this angel sent from heaven,
I only want with you to hold, Steven our Steven.

Futility 1 Sept 1991

The day I will never forget, At least we had
the family around whilst Eva quietly slipped
away. After 27 years? where do I go from here ?

My dearest love please to watch over,
This shell of a man left behind,
Be with me in deed and at times when I need
You to bolster my heart, and my mind,
How I miss you, I just can't engender,
Things we should have, together attained,
Gone our love Oh! so precious, so tender,
It's the why that cannot be explained,
It's so wrong to be here now without you,
It's so hard to find reasons to live,
So unfair of the cancer that took you
When we still had a lifetime to give,
Alone I'm so brim full of memories,
Their reason has fritted and died,
And I wake, to find tears on my pillow,
To find that's another night cried.

Amazing Maze

A hardy strain of Sweetcorn has been developed
which will grow to a good height 6ft which will
enable the farmer to rely on it for winter fodder,
Unfortunately this crop requires to be grown under
a starter sheet of clear foil, which should be
biodegradable.

Late April to May, is the time that you see,
Neat rows of transparent, fields covered they be,
It used to be grass, then rape became gold,
Now this new agriproduct has taken a hold.

Varied the use of this crop there can be,
It's maize, forms a maze, that's amazing to see,
If pruned when an infant, it won't grow to full height,
But left unamended, would hide you from sight.

By selectively shearing the route that, pre-planned,
Results in a pattern, imposed on the land,
The larger the area first planted and foiled,
Enables more complex the pattern revealed.

Admission be charged, to traverse the route,
But a flag must be carried, please rescue, salute,
When walked to a standstill, the crop fully formed,
To be cut and part shredded, and finally homed.

As silage to supplement the long winter feeds,
Enables the farmer to fulfil his stock's needs,
Lets hope the transparent is degradable Bio,
If not, it's pollutant, and surely must go.

Wasps

The nest was spherical and made out of wood pulp
chewed up wood by different wasps who then spit
the pulp in layers forming strata of layers in arc
shapes which interlock giving the nest its strength,
very delicate, very dangerous.

Filling the bird feeder, whilst in my back shed,
I was conscious of buzzing, over my head,
Stood still and listened, located the sound,
It came from some boxes, see, here's what I found.

Bees,Wasps, Hover flies, and Bumble bees,
All do good for our flowers and trees,
The pollen they carry is the seed of life,
The Wasp seems a loner, a creator of strife.

Some Wasps live alone, in a solitary state,
Whilst others unite and a house they create,
By chewing at wood, till they can't eat no more,
Then home to their nest where they spit up and pour.

Constructed from paper, see all of the layers,
Each colour is made by a different stayer,
The layers form a barrier, to keep out the cold,
The inside, a comb which their eggs it will hold.

If ever you find, when you're out on your own,
A nest, much like this, then please leave it alone,
Wasps can get angry, they fight as a swarm,
A wasp sting will hurt, but a lot will do real harm.

But wasps are our friends, just like bees and more.
They carry pollen to add to the score
Of flowers and crops which we humans need.
So thanks to all wasps, just go on, but take heed.

Cup Final (Covid)

The Cup Final played without spectators, written in such a way as to imply that I knew nowt about the game or the emotion that the sport generated in the north of England.

Leeds against Salford, the best of the rest,
Eighty minutes on the pitch, each man will give his best,
Each of the thirteen chaps a champing, and determined not to fall,
You've had your summertime rest, now's the time to use the ball.

The whistle blows, the ball soars and every heart takes flight,
The pitch is lined across its width, each strip they need to fight,
Six tackles limit each team's turn, to wrest against the foe,
With half a dozen in reply, rescind the yardage go.

Divided slices of the pitch, each loss and gain a measure,
Each segment be it lost or gained will tension raise to treasure,
The boundary lines at either end wherein the goals are founded,
Remain the ultimate line to cross, beyond the ball be grounded.

To score and convert successfully the try object intent,
When points be scored for touchdown ball, beyond the line be sent,
Another score be added more if 'tween the H converted,
Full eighty minutes span hand-to-hand as pressure unrelented.

'Till hands do shake opponents take, the best of pals frequent,
The Covid Rule "Spectator Ban" so health and safety founded,
The game was played, the league fulfilled, the "Cup winners" awarded.
Spectatorless sport the players didn't notice, I think, I hope.

Coronavirus 2020

We've had the new election, a premier has been picked.
It wasn't who I wanted, but the chaff has all been kicked,
He started to make progress, to set the world to rights,
But miles away in China, grew medical based frights,
The Coronavirus virus has escaped, its deadly run to spread
With two weeks incubation, from fit to choking dead.

Outbreaks the whole world over Japan to U.S.A.
Spread mainly via aircraft, so what else can I say
Patients dying in their hundreds. No vaccines could we send.
With which to fight our quarter, a treatment that would mend.
The first week cost a thousand, scattered wildly o'er the world.
Now many more have fallen, where Coronavirus has been hurled.

No public place is open, no football, film, or dance.
The coffee bars have closed, we each must take our chance.
Supermarkets ration time, 'tween OAP and NHS.
Bus and train services, cut to half, or even less,
Public parks and beaches are forbidden for to roam,
and gatherings of three people. Barred, unless you are at home.

Newsflash as of Friday. the PM has the lurgy, and so does half his team
Despite the firm constrictions, it spreads so well it seems.
They're working on a vaccine, which will make all immune.
At the rate of its contagion, it needs to get here soon.
The costs it is incurring, in cash, and angst, and fear.
Disrupts the whole life cycle, for many coming year.

Lockdown's been in force now, three weeks or is it four?
With pills and grocery orders, delivered to your door,
The hospitals are bloated, and care homes full to burst,
It's lasting for so long now, far more than was rehearsed,
The cafes are in lockdown, and all the bars are shut,
Factories and building, no work, no sales, kaput.

The dole and other payments, DHS and unemploy,
Are paying out their moneys, the bank rate it destroy,
This Viro's spread via vapour, we must stay yards apart,
A tickle in the airways a racking cough ensue,
With rapid raise in temperature, much worse than common flu,
The lungs with phlegm congested, survival rate is phew!

Trump has found the answer, it's well within our reach,
Schools no more to be boycott, so back you go. and teach,
Also it means you can retain your picnic on the beach,
Resume your football playing, and churches fill, beseech,
We'll all make new arrangements, his proposal is to each,
If we should do, as he suggest, inject ourselves with bleach.

Coronavirus virus19

C   China the source of Virus 19, responded to the need,
      Built two hospitals, isolated, treated, segregated, freed.

O   Outbreak spread rapidly throughout the world,
      Mainly by aircraft, by which passengers hurled.

R   Range of contagion, via vapour, spittle, and sweat.
      Two metres apart, no less, then showered you'll get.

O   Orient, it rapidly spread, to Japan and Vietnam.
      Where victims and carriers, they isolated them.

N   Nowhere be safe 'cause of the vast varied coverage,
      By individual travel, and commercial carriage.

A   Australians are sure of the source of their infection.
      Passengers arrived, disembarked, with no medical inspection.

V   Vaccination is being researched throughout the world.
      Universities and labs, worldwide are enrolled.

I   Immunity is granted to those persons who.
      Have previously suffered, a bout of 19 type flu.

R   Stature, age, gender, or race, cannot avoid the viro's pace.
      Infection attacks without thought or regard for colour of face.

U   Unknown as yet, the worlds total deaths that stand.
      Which can be attributed to this viro's hand.

S   Survival from infection needs complete PPE.
      Patients on respiration, have all the help that can be.

V   Virus - an infective agent smaller than a micro organism.
      Requiring living cells to enable its multiplication.

I   Infection induces the lungs to express,
      The virus causes bleeding and phlegm.

R   Respiration, the requirement for artificial respiration to aid
      the breathing of, severely infected invalids.

U   Undertakers are burying the dead in common graves.
      In groups at a time for the costs that it saves.

S   Selective, old above young, gross above slight.
      Coloured in origin, above european white.

19   Total WORLD DEAD 2,432,014   CONTAMINATED   110,132,703
     DATE Feb 17,2021

Ena Hutchinson

Waiting to Sing

They have closed all the shops
my friend said in horror,
the gym and the cinemas too.
I can't go to Church or visit
my friends as I used to do.
Guess what? They've just shut the Zoo!

What is the problem?
Why are the streets so empty and bare?
Then early evening... the News reveals all
COVID 19 has arrived on our shores.

Throughout 2020 the whole world has been
Locked in, Locked out and Locked down again
Let's Hope that we can all remain sane.

Hope! Hope! is a wonderful thing,
Scientists working long into the night,
Producing a Vaccine the end is in sight.
When that thankfully happens
                          the whole world will sing.

Picture of my Birthday celebrations
– notice the empty seats

The Knapp on the doorstep

The Knapp is the local name for the Motte and Double Bailey 'Castle Pulverbatch' historic remains in Shropshire

Walking the Knapp one blustery day
My very young grandson beside me, did say,
What is the wind - Where is it from...
and grandma, Where does it go?

"Good question Jack - It's a wonder of nature
in God's wonderful world."

As we climbed to the top, Long Mynd came in sight
The wind was blowing with all of its might.
The wind's like God's Spirit it's all around,
Reach out to catch it, all you hear is the sound

The rustle of leaves as it blows through the trees,
The flower heads nod and dance in the breeze.
If it blusters and catches you unawares
It will playfully push you and pull you about

and when it is stronger it'll stop you
and hold you
as you try to stride out.

The Spirit of God can be just like the wind,
not something you see ... yet can be found.
There can be silences, never a sound,
a whisper, yet you can sense something near.
Just like the wind in the trees gently blowing,
caressing you just like the leaves,
leaving you glowing.

There are times when the wind, very strong
bends the bough
shaking us up to be stronger, just as it is now.

The Knapp and the farm lane Jack and Grandad
often would roam.
Rucksack on back, with a mission; to collect
fallen branches and twigs to take home.
These were the kindling that would light the
living room fire,
where later we would all gather round.
Playing games on the floor or reading a book
not making a sound.
These precious moments so special to capture,
looking back, Oh so brief, but what rapture.

Bringing back memories once more,
the days before Covid 19 that's for sure.
Grandad not with us: he had crossed o'er the shore.

Visiting Shropshire to be with the family once more,
Jack, now a confident business man, took me aside,
"How would you like to go for ride and walk up the Knapp
How lovely, the two of us! "Yes" I replied.

Wrapping up warm Jack took us there in the car,
they had moved nearer town but it wasn't too far.
Thrilled to be looking again at Long Mynd
There's a seat now to sit and pause as you climb.
The Knapp's not very high but it really is steep.
Such a wonderful morning - more memories to keep.

Ruth Kershaw

SONG OF HOPE

*"Through the night of doubt and sorrow"**

Present pestilence Covid 19
Many forerunners with hope of deliverance
All ending, sooner or later,
In the same, yet altered, world.
As this one will.

"Onward goes the pilgrim band"

Faith, Hope and Love – the eternal three.
Hope lifting us on her shoulders
To glimpse a better time beyond
Where all manner of things shall be well.

"Singing songs of expectation"

Stay positive, pause and plan...
A planet to save
Peace to establish.
Personal wants...

"Marching to the promised land"

In my lonely lockdown
I think of the suffering in (and of) the world,
As I wait for the library to open
And yearn to touch and sing.

*Verse Bernhardt Severin Ingerman 1789 -1862
Tr. By Sabine Baring-Gold 1834 - 1924

October 2020

`ARE WE NEARLY THERE'

Off we go – passengers four small sons
Excited at first,
All too soon restless and fidgety.
One of them is sick!
They wail,
`Are we nearly there?'

Once travelling from north to south
We journeyed overnight.
Never again. They slept, we didn't.
On the beach next day
Shattered adults, lively boys
Yes, we were there!

These sons drive me now.
Treats planned with love and care.
Twisty lanes to see this and that.
Tea promised at the end.
Soon I need a comfort stop.
Hurry – get us there!

It helps when you know the way.
Sometimes traffic jams, diversions, hold ups
Delay arrival time.
Eventually, we do get there.

In 2020 Covid19 turned life upside down.
Vicious, virulent pushing the world to lockdown,
Scientists search for exits.
Vaccines found, hope kindled
Oh pray
We are `nearly there'.

January 2021

THE CUMBRIA CYCLE WAY

(Sponsored 280 mile peddle in 1992 for a church in Sierra Leone.)

The landside around Cumbria
Rugged and exciting.
The coastal, spying Isle of Man,
Is equally inviting.

It started well, the day was fine,
Two biddies on their bikes
Embarked upon the Cycle Way,
Past fields and dells and pikes.

Kirkby Stephen our first bedding,
A night with Ruth's good friend.
We peddled on through Appleby.
Her house was round a bend.

In Mallerstang the road was steep.
Sedbergh – free wheel down
And on to Kirkby Lonsdale
A friendly market town

Next, early start for Ulverston
Hutton Roof, and soon the sands,
At Arnside had ace fish and chips
Then on to welcoming hands.

Away by eight – St Bees tonight – Oh,
Ambition knows no bounds,
Barrow, Millom, Ravenglass –
The wheels do umpteen rounds.

Sellafield pulled our spirits down,
A controversial site,
Then we cheered up through Ravenglass
And by St Bees felt bright.

We lingered on the beach a while,
Then headed north and on.
A strong headwind frustrated us
Energy up and gone.

The wheels they still go round and round,
If now a trifle slow
The bells keep on with ring-a-ding.
We ought to stop, you know!

Struggling to Silloth we plough on.
A rest day is a must.
Bottoms and legs are very sore.
Unless we stop we bust!

The last day - back to Brampton now.
We should be home for tea.
Abbeytown, Anthorn, dear Carlisle.
We've made it – wow, yippee!!

Yet still the bells go ring-a-ding
The wheels still round and round.
Our sponsors are awaiting us –
There's money to be found!

2121

THE GIFT OF THE GAP

Some take a 'gap year'
A break from routine.
Time to sort things out,
Maybe travel
Or just relax
And plan ahead.

The skiffle celebrated
Fifteen mile Appalachian cleft
America's first Gateway to the West -
The Cumberland Gap –
Allows migration
For nature and mankind.

2020 gave a gap
So unwelcome
Yet an interval in which
To learn and plan towards
A better tomorrow.
May this too
Be a gift of a gap.

2021

Travelling on – A series of Haikus

Ways

Ocean, sky, terrain
Transport when travelling far.
Choose land, sea or air.

Boats

River, ocean, stream
Take ferry, ship, canoe or a
Slow boat to China

Airborne

Up. Drinks, food, and films.
Then, `Fasten your belts for down.'
Hope for smooth landing.

Jan-Feb 2021

ICONIC RAILWAY

In 19th century Midland undertook the construction of a route between England and Scotland. 1895 saw the opening for freight and then soon passengers of the Settle – Carlisle section. Freight continues and passenger numbers have increased – commuters, shoppers, tourists, football supporters, day trippers, walkers and so on enjoying its splendour and history. I am a volunteer on-train-guide – working Saturdays.

A journey from Carlisle to Settle
Can be done on a bike,
Or a very long hike,
By road in the car,
But better by far –
Let the train take the strain.

Let me show you the sights
(Maybe sell you a book)
As we glide by the lush River Eden
With hedges and trees, livestock that please
Climbing near to its source
When we pass Hell Gill Force.

On our left the Pennines,
Lake district fells to the right,
My party is thrilling
To vistas around us
As Appleby comes into sight.

The trolley rolls on –
Coffee shortbread and more.
Smardale from high up we view.
Kirkby Stephen comes next,
Mallerstang with Wild Boar.
Ramblers will leave the train soon.

The platform sits two miles from the town,
Dent, further, on even more.
This station claims height over all,
A long tunnel connects us to
Famed Ribblehead,
Navvy settlement, Viaduct,
Head of our next valley.

Grey stones here replace the red
Limestone cliffs and pavements
The infant Ribble splashes down
Hundreds on The Three Peak Walk,
Sponsored, have made this place
A honey-pot for charity.

Settle, welcome destination.
A good break here to eat, explore
Take a walk or stay close by.
Here is the signal box, the shop and books,
The Water Tower is now a home
Welcoming travellers to its grounds.

All safely on board, and off again,
Scenery still stunning.
Time to dwell on extra things.
Crisis: Beeching v Portillo,
Friends Of The Line, communities,
Volunteers, striving hard to save.

Architecture, colour schemes,
Gardens, platforms, offers,
Where to go from here,
History in the landscape.
Here is the trolley, back again,
And yes, she does have beer!

My party (gelled) is chatting.
Such a very good day,
"Must keep in touch, meet up again.
A Northern line runs round the coast..."
And I am loathe to see them go –
Everyone with a book.

2021

"BUS PASS BRITAIN"
– Brandt 2011

The fire alarm is blaring - we have to get out now,
Grab what we can as to the assembly point we go.
I snatch my purse; it holds
My bus pass and my cards,
Hoping this is just a practice,
But then you never know.

Bus Pass Britain gives the routes
Of fifty fantastic journeys
South to North then West and East,
Some linking for a longer ride –
Brandt's amazing travel guide.
Come, dip into its pages.

Retirement age allows a pass,
Times restrict its use.
Soon, up and ready, off we head
To hills and coast,
What tempts us most
Or shopping days instead.

Turn the pages to find
The route by me (I got a fee!)
Penrith to Patterdale.
Hop off then later on again
To walk, eat or view
Sights so stunning and new.

Lockdown travel, so frustrating;
Sit far apart and wear a mask.
No longer roam, just stay at home,
Essential journeys only.
Still, time to plan for when we can
Go out once again more freely.

Ah, smoke from a toaster
Triggered the switch to the loud alarm.
We heave a sigh,
Give a grin as
We trundle back in.
Purses in hand, jubilant band.

STAGECOACH 77/77A

*A circular route that goes over Honister and
Whinlatter passes from Keswick.*

At the tail end of a very long queue she glanced
around for her friend. Was it allowed to keep a
place? These ramblers look tough. Will they all
get on? Ah, here comes Erica and the single-
decker too. The passengers shuffle on and then a
straining dog followed by its panting owner ("Hey,
steady on – remember I'm at the end of this lead!")
They nod at him. He's from their town. This
regular service provides a choice of off and on stay
to return in an hour and more.

A very tight squeeze with folk on knees and
standing we peer at the view until Stair where a
rambling party alights to climb Cat Bells.
Contouring high the vista opens up and thrills. A
blue garage door shows where Hugh Walpole lived
and then St. Olaphs with the dog toothed window
surrounds tells us we are now in Grange. Joan is
on a trip down memory lane and needs to share.

"This bridge marks where they drowned a witch."

"That cottage wall is where (long years ago) the
lady of the house would place a teapot to ask
the driver to stop."

As they passed The Glaramara Centre "When I
was a student I often worked there."

Seatoller – more walkers leave, passengers
spread out to glimpse ghyll scramblers below
conquer the steepest of rapids. Up, up and on
we go until the Youth Hostel and the Mine come
into view. When misty this is an awesome and
desolate spot. Today is fine and clear.
The Mine is closed, yet open anew. Museum, café,
shop, a track up to the cave with more
ambitious plans in mind.

A ZIP WIRE! What? Oh surely not. We'll see.

Gatesgarth, Buttermere; lake and village.
Gentler walks here, cafes and inns. Some get
off whilst others climb on. Our two find time
for an ice-cream.

Crummock Water now and Joan is at it again,
"There is the path into Rannerdale for the blue
bells. An ancient crab apple there too."

On and past Lorton, "We lived there when the boys
were small"

Well wooded Whinlater twists and turns. Erica
seizes her chance and shouts, "On the C2C Cycle
Way I peddled up here!!" Some of the passengers
would like to cheer! A halt at the Centre, splendid
and new, offering adventure, trails a shop and café
too. The man and the dog are heading that way.
Then down to a huge turning space, for a camera
stop.

Joan chimes up once more, "This was my dad's
favourite view". Skiddaw spreads wide arms to
greet. Once scorned as a `grandmother's
mountain' Joan has reached that age now. It's her
favourite, one of the few left she can do! The bus
negotiates Braithwaite via the narrows, then full
speed to Keswick where it starts off again.

Erica asks, "Joan do you think that you can
remember a good place to eat?"

.

.

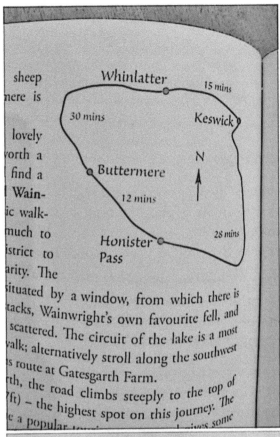

sheep
here is

lovely
worth a
find a
Wain-
ic walk-
much to
istrict to
arity. The
situated by a window, from which there is
tacks, Wainwright's own favourite fell, and
scattered. The circuit of the lake is a most
walk; alternatively stroll along the southwest
s route at Gatesgarth Farm.
rth, the road climbs steeply to the top of
ft) – the highest spot on this journey. The
e a popular t... ... ...ives some

John S Langley

*This contribution to the Anthology is a sequence of poems
linked by the theme of 'life's journey' from 'Beginnings'
to 'Time to Leave' but then ending with the idea of
continuity, one life following another – and long may it
continue!*

Beginnings

New sounds, new eyes, new sights
amidst the smells of an old world
form an awakening, a sparking
of synapses that hold a thought of life.

Each thing a new revelation
before sounds become words before
faces harden into people with different smells
(some bought some eau naturelle).

Not yet aware of your own identity
crying for comfort or food or love driven
on by instinct and an inbuilt engine
growing bone, sinew, flesh and blood, riding

a wave, an arching arrow of time without wings
moving in an irreversible trajectory
gathering strength to lift a heavy head
to push, to roll, with repeated purpose

to sit as if sitting were something always known
to smile up into faces when lying on your belly
to kneel, to push, to slip and try again, to stretch
and in stretching to fall and cry and be picked up

and over days not knowing how
to start to crawl, new things in reach
no turning back...

        ...nothing is safe now.

Revelations

When you watch young children discovering their
world for the first time you can see the surprise and
the wonder at each new discovery – I sometimes wish
we did not so easily grow out of this…

Can this ever have been seen before
or felt the way I feel it
surely this is new to all the world
and nothing that has gone before
can ever have come close.

These eyes that I now see through
must bring new revelations
how can I describe what I now know
in words that I have not yet learnt
beneath a sky of consternations.

Oh give me breath and give me means
to share these things I see
with these others who hold me close
who seem to want to keep me safe
and bounce me on their knee.

(An extract from a piece of Textile Art by a very talented artist called Janet C. Langley – who happens, by sheer coincidence, to also be my wife.)

Trial and Terror

*This poem is based on a real-life (or near death)
experience of my own – we seem to need to learn by
doing things for ourselves, by trial and error – although I
wouldn't recommend this particular experiment.*

The rattle-cart was a glorious thing
four pram wheels and an orange crate
designed for speed like it had wings
it sped down the hill till it came to a gate

Oh calamity, calamity!
I wish we'd put in some brakes
we might have stayed right where we were
instead of shooting through the air
and rolling, tumbling, and then crashing
in a bedraggled state

The bruises they would heal
after going through the colours
the cuts would seal to scars
that we could show to others

there was pride that we'd come through it
survived the helter-skelter
with so little damage to ourselves
though 'twas fatal for the rattle-cart

One wheel we never found
though we really searched around
That cart it taught us an awful lot
and such knowledge we put in the pot
together with string and super-glue
as we began to design Mark 2!

*An example from the internet of a similarly
dangerous vehicle – although this one has
a brake!*

Dive Right In

The water was cold, freezing cold
  up to my thin goose-pimpled thighs
    and I froze not knowing whether
     the lesser evil was to dive
       in or climb out onto dry land.

        My father and brother had braved
         the sea, splashing salt water in
          white trails of laughter and shouting
          that I should jump in and join them
          that *'It's alright once you're all in.'*

        I stretched out my spindly arms tucked
        my head like an olympian
       and bent forward. My heart said jump
       my head said don't be so stupid
       it's freezing, it's bad enough stood

     here, on the edge of decision.
     Dad shouted it was up to me.
     I could jump in or get out and
    wait on the beach, kicking sand and
    drying off. I took the challenge

    braced myself, determined this time...

***

***

I can see myself as I look
back on that scared kid at
that pivotal moment. To do
or to retreat, to dream.
I close my eyes and I see that...

***

And now, when there are choices to
be made, when there are dreams to chase
I think of that small boy, who did
not jump and I jump because

I understand the difference

between the shock of ice cold water
and waiting on the beach

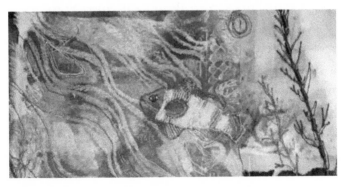

*(Extract from another piece of original Textile Art by
the same talented artist.)*

93

Moving on

*It seems to me that we live our lives on the edge
between past and future increasingly weighed down
with the experiences and memories we accumulate –
we might believe we have trod the path we set for
ourselves or can plan the way ahead but it doesn't take
much to change all that...*

Cat-eye bright the morning, the path made purple
by rut-filled reflection, leaf-dewed litter
that shimmers in the haze

Behind (where I do not look) a deeper darkness lowers
seeps through pores, flows from shadow-wrinkled bark
to cloud my over-active memory

and I, what there is still of me, stands here between
on the knife edge, neither departed nor arrived
knowing I must take an unknowable next step

and as I strive to see my way, to plan ahead
as if I could, I know that it but takes a breath
a rustle midst the drying leaves
to redirect the path I see
and alter all before.

Snakes

Snakes are an example of something that is not at the top of everybody's 'My Favourite Things' list. I have always had a healthy respect for them and this experience did nothing to change that.

I thought snakes were slithery as most people say
but one fine day when I was at the zoo someone said 'Hey'
and I said, 'Me?' and she said 'Yes, you.
Do you want to handle a snake?
I'll put it round your neck
It's only an anaconda.'
and I thought, 'What the heck.'

It was heavy with splodgy markings and over three feet long
with an evil eye, a darting tongue, and I thought that it would pon
but it didn't smell at all, it obviously kept very clean
though when she started to put it on I wasn't very keen.

'Wait just a minute,' I said out loud, 'are you sure that this is safe
'Oh, just about,' the Keeper said, 'As long as you don't make
... any sudden moves, or shout, or scream, as that might only scar
and when it's scared it could play up, I mean you couldn't blame i

u're putting it around my neck?' I said, with eyes now open wide
', yes, I suppose,' the Keeper said, 'but I'll be here at your side.'
h good,' I said though not convinced, but before I could say more
e'd placed the snake around my neck and I just thought, 'Oh, cor,
I going to try to love this snake as it really would be a shame
t started to tighten around my neck with only me to blame.'

rough my hands I could feel its strength and I tried to keep it happy
lidn't move, I didn't flinch, I tried to be a brave strong chappy
ow's that?' the Keeper asked, 'She's really quite a dear,
e'll be calm and gentle as could be if you don't show any fear.'
ook her words as gospel, held my breath and stood real still
e snake just lay there languid as if testing my strength and will.

ter an eternity of seconds the Keeper said 'That will do'
d lifted the snake right off me and returned me to life anew
ho wants to be next?' she said with a smile
d a small girl raised her hand
lid not watch what happened next...
                    ... as it might not have gone as planned!

I walked back to meet my son
Proud at what I'd achieved
'How was it Dad?' he said to me 'You looked terrified.'
'Terrified!' I said to him, 'Oh no, that was concentration
I didn't want to scare the thing, I was enjoying the sensation
of having a live snake round my neck
a big snake made of muscle
a snake that could crush the life out of a pig
a snake that...'

For some reason he had started to chuckle
as the memory started to make my knees buckle
so I sat down beside him as white as a sheet
said. 'If you promise your silence I'll give you a treat.'
but he only laughed more and louder at that
and said 'Mum's going to love our very next chat
when I tell her about how you met with a snake
and the photos I took a real story will make.'

I paused to think...

'How about an ice cream?' I said in reply
at least that would give me the time to think why
I'd done it at all – and then I remembered
I'd wanted to know if snakes
were slippery or wet
and now I knew it was like winning a bet
I'd found out that they're actually dry...
...and very strong...
and if you want to check
it's better not to do it
by wearing one round your neck.

They just don't seem that friendly to me.

Keeping the Flame Alive

Memories are important things and Scotland
holds a place in my heart for lots of reasons.

It was only the other night
I added two logs to the fire
watched them catch light
lick with flame and rise

yellow, orange, flickering red
alive with an unsteady steadiness
wrapped in wisps of smoke that reach
and take my hand in readiness

to lead me gently upwards
and backwards, embracing me
in remembered scents
of half-forgotten times

back to the hills and the heather
the call of the skittering grouse
the purples, greens and amber
far from this stone built house

to wash in the tumbling waters
beneath a blue-splashed sky
to walk the high hills and deep valleys
without always wondering 'Why?'

I saw it all in memory
while the flames they twisted and turned
and I who sat there humbly
watched the logs until they'd burned.

Music to My Ears

Memories can be triggered by the strangest
things and at the strangest times... and
certainly music is one of those triggers. How
many of us have not had (or still have) a
record player of some description in our lives?

The needle descends
slips neatly
into a vinyl groove
that rotates
at 33 and a third
revolutions
per minute
magically
producing music

Amplified
it reaches out
into past Christmases
birthdays
celebrations
and quieter moments
like this one
a fresh communion
with an old rhythm
"Unforgettable
that's what you are..."

We used to have a Stereo Cabinet like this – I think our record collection amounted to about 6 albums and 4 singles (One being 'Little White Bull').

Last Cast?

*Maybe this isn't everybody's cup of tea but I like to go
fishing. I don't go often but when I do the best
occasions are when I go along with friends. Memories
are made of times like these and I don't know when
the next or last such occasion will be - who ever does?*

Line running out in the evening light
yellow-orange, a mirror pool
mozzies biting, eyes focused
on the final cast of a long day
that skittles over the glassy surface
dry fly, brown, light, spindly
daddy long legs

I let it settle, let it settle
the final cast, of a day with friends
coffee from flasks on the river bank
pre-packed sandwiches
cheese, egg, tomato
easy on the mayo

I let it settle, let it settle
easy now, easy
and start the slow retrieve
the last cast of the day
almost ready to pack up
no fish, but fond memories

But then! ... a rise
a fish breaks the surface
takes the fly

I wait a second
1, 2, 3
strike
the line goes taut

the fish pulls and runs
keep the line tight
give a little
take a little
play the fish
respect the fight
take your time
and slowly
slowly
bring it in

A friend handles the net
as the fish is coaxed a little nearer
this way
then away
let it run
back again
just a little more
just a little closer
Now!
And the net is lifted
full with its glittering prize
Well done
A brown trout

Look how beautifully marked
silver backed, yellow under
brown and red spotted
gasping for breath
Careful!

And with wet hands
important that the hands are wet
I remove the hook
a quick photo
and ease it back
held only for a moment
letting the fish get its bearings
then release
and with a flick of its tail
it disappears
back into the darkening waters.

And later we ask
Why do we do it?
spend all day
trying to catch something
we then release
Another creature
a living thing
disturbed for a moment
from its natural rhythm.

The reasons are too complicated
A communing with nature
A day with friends

Some fresh air
and exercise
A chase, a hunt, a catch
A mental recharge
An innate memory?

It is too much
too difficult to say
so we say too little
and are just thankful
thankful
and hope that there might be a time
when we will do it all again.

The fishing
spot

THE FISH !

Walking the Tide-line

*Tidelands represent a rise and fall, the incoming and
outgoing of tidal waters, the idea of perpetual change
amidst predictable cycles, a metaphor for each of us
individually as well as collectively as a species that
lives within a rotating wheel of time.*

Blue waves beneath a blue sky
crack open white and push grain
against grain, grinding the sand
before rustling back to an incoming tide

From above the birds spear into the sea
or ride the tightrope of the wind
looking, attentive for the next opportunity
far travelled yet far to go

Dogs bark and splash, rush, return
demand a new throw, another rush
and gather sand in leaping paws
and rolling matted hair

Along the tide-line there are footprints
large, small, shod, barefoot
sharp of outline until
the next wave pushes through

and washes clean, levels up
treating all the same
together with the spilled ice cream
disappearing back into a greater whole
to be ready... for another tide.

Time to Leave

Departures can hurt. Even when you know they have to happen, even when they're the right and proper thing to happen, even when the time is right... it still isn't easy.

It seems like you've only just arrived
when I know it's time for you to go
I'll always remember how we tried
to make the most of it, and so

I wish you well upon your way
and hope to meet some other day

Will we be different people then?
Our paths no longer parallel
and will you still remember when
I stood here and wished you well

with hidden tears behind my eyes
knowing your journey had just begun
trying to smile without telling lies
knowing part of the race had been run

You have forever changed my life
in ways I never could have thought
and now our lives will change again
and I wish you well
I love you and I wish you well.

I took this photo on a snowy day in Feb 2021 and the tracks seemed to me to symbolise the idea of travelling – arriving and departing leaving temporary tracks as a marker of the journey...

At the Cave Mouth

*The idea of this poem is to give an impression of how
eras layer one upon another, and how we strive in our
different ways to leave a mark.*

At the cave mouth
the smell of rain
the softened landscape
like a memory recalled
after too long an absence.

She looks out on infinity
her fingers matted, coated
her palms smeared with red ochre
yellow umber
ground fine from old earth
mixed, bound and newly blown.

The cave wall behind her is lit red
by the evening sun
the stone wall glistens with new art
not yet dry
that attempts to tell a story
or ask a question
or simply leave a mark.

Now who stands at the cave mouth?
The artist is gone but the art remains
the rain still falls
the sky teeters
but has not yet fallen
upon our heads.

I Saw a Swallow Fledge

*In some years swallows nest in our porch, surviving
all the comings and goings, making a mess,
determined to produce the next generation and get
them flying before they have to leave. Even so, being
able to witness a 'first launch' was a unique
experience.*

I saw a swallow fledge
that unique moment

After days and days
of wondering if
there were anything in the nest
we see a trepidatious movement
a fleeting glimpse of punk-spiked heads

Wide, yellow, gaping mouths
at the nest's rim
that rise in raucous cacophony
at the return of a parent
bearing fresh food

"Feed me!"
"No me!"
"Over here!"
"Don't miss me!"

Dishevelled but with glistening eyes
as the poop starts to pile
underneath the nest
and a diet of flies
is converted to bone
to muscle and sinew
to colour and feathers

There were barren days of rain
that slowed growth
increased the risk of abandonment
but in time
dry gaps
spawning new hatches
providing enough sources
of nourishment

There were also days of sun and plenty
of overfilling, overflowing
and speedy growth
four chicks fast out-growing
the mud-made nest

Then... one of the chicks
on a bright morning
perched on the edge
formed enough
though still with a wide gape
and tufts between its feathers
stood

Is it too soon?

a pause
a leaning forward
head first
a testing of wings
a stretching
an unsure start

A launch!

a leaving of the nest
a frantic beating of wings
a hovering panic
a landing
on an adjacent ledge

The next few days
bring surges of confidence
competence
pre-destined
pre-designed
preparing to dive
into an unknown fate
to swoop and to be held aloft
to climb into the sky
scared, euphoric
timely

I saw a swallow fledge
what a privilege.

This photo is of the swallows nesting in our porch – the nest is built around a light fitting – it's taken a little before (but not long before) the time of fledging.

Doreen Moscrop

Our Holiday during Lockdown

Today we went on holiday around the Irish coast,
from Dublin to Stillorgan, there to meet our host,
Dinner, Bed and Breakfast then across the Central Plain
by Limerick to Killarney on the wild Atlantic main.

Another hotel, fabulous food then back upon the coach
Tralee to The Dingle Peninsula, beaches and cliffs encroach
Return in time for dinner, then next morning travel scene
To Muckross House, ride the jaunty cars and cruise upon Lough Lean

Next comes the Ring of Kerry, a hundred miles of awe
Steep mountains, rugged coastline, so much to explore
green fields, historic houses and glacial lakes abound
welcoming towns and villages round every bend we found.

Homeward bound via Cashel, an historical Heritage city
we say goodbye to Ireland and their fine hospitality
by Larne to Cairnryan back across the Irish Sea
Now I'll put away the brochure and put the kettle on for tea.

A Mardale Christmas

Did voices ring with Christmas cheer
from the Old Dun Bull where every year
the Shepherds Meet had passed once more,
from neighbouring vales the huntsmen came
bright lights from every window shone.
So quiet now when all hast gone.

Did carols echo from inside
the little church that stood with pride
beneath those ancient spreading yews,
with frost and snow upon the ground
ice crystals stilled the dancing waves
below Chapel Hill slept silent graves.

Did children's laughter ring around
the little school on Whelter Sound
gazing upwards to Castle Crag,
where buzzards flew and eagles called
no thoughts all peace would soon have flown
this sheltered life they'd always known.

Did angels tread this way before
when through the dale sharp winds did roar
bringing peace and hope to everyone,
before the flood their valley stole
from 'neath the waves a voice did cry,
but through the silence came no reply.

THE BIG QUESTION

*I sat down and composed this poem after
a phone call to a friend who loves the
countryside as much as I do and has been
isolated since March.*

When?
When will you come and walk with me,
where can we go, what shall we see?
This plague decrees we stroll alone
Our world this isolation's never known.

When will you come and drive away
to hills and dales where we can stay?
For now at home I only dream
I take your hand to cross the stream.

When will you come and sit a while
on cool grey stone or foot-worn stile?
Without two metres in between,
no mask, your smile so clearly seen.

When will you come and take my arm,
no empty space, a healing balm?
From humankind I'm kept apart,
no comforting hold to warm my heart.

When will you come and stay once more,
have time to stravaig a Lakeland shore?
Visit friends and family we hold so dear,
old haunts to explore, no pandemic to fear?

Cumbria August 2020

Innominate Tarn

How will my heart remember you
    what picture engraved in my mind
    your dark rocky tor surrounding
    a quiet jewel unrefined.
The ways I trod to find you
    now quiet, the quarries long dead
    the scars of toil, many days past
    in purple heather now bespread.
Through a tangle of tall bracken
    past peaty pools, dark and still
    this urgent need to be with you
    a fierce yearning to fulfil.
You need no name to hold my love
    clear waters shall bear my bier
    your shores shall be my resting place
    at close of life's frontier.

Blea Tarn – Eskdale

High above the valley where the
    little train does run.
Its waters lie behind a combe to
    catch the early sun.
With rocky shores around the bays
    tall gentle swaying reeds
Boulders throw deep shadows where the
    bright blue dragonfly feeds.

The sense of peace and calmness that
    comes of a fleeting stay
A welcome pause to the weary traveller
    going on his way.
The tarn spills cool clear waters
    into the Esk below.
On its ever meandering journey to
    the solway it will flow.

The Carpets of Autumn

The summer's done, the heat long gone
    the frost now on the ground
in country lane, on open plain
    a lake with reeds around.
The trees are shorn, their branches torn
    their leaves they cann't hold
from green to brown come tumbling down
    bright circles of red and gold.
In valleys deep, when sides rise steep
    forests patchwork in colours serene
a pale green haze with brown and beige
    strange designs in every dene
steep mountain slope, the long dead stope
    sun dried bracken bursting red
strong heathers fade, then mists invade
    dark clouds their rain to shed.
The heavens teem, the rushing stream
    silver ribbons tumbling down
the lakes are filled, reflections frilled
    dead reeds stand tall and brown.
The days are wan, the bright lights gone
    skies herald approaching night
then snowflakes fall to blanket all
    in a carpet of winter white

When 'Covid' came to our Town

When the covid plague hit our small town,
Shops, cafes and hairdressers had to close.
A lockdown kept us all inside.
Total isolation the powers did impose.
Then came the decree the small outlets to open,
Time to venture out, shopping to start
A mask must be worn, no welcoming smile
social distance maintained. Keep 2 metres apart.
Out came the sleeping sewing machine.
Face coverings to make and design.
Checked ones, spotty ones and some in dark blue
soft washable cotton to hang on the line.

Monday morning, my first forage out
half a mile walk, a newspaper to buy
good for one's health, people to meet.
I was leaving the house when I heard my wife cry
"Don't forget your mask"
The newsagents was quiet, the queue quite short
'only one person in the shop at a time' on display.
I soon had my purchase under my arm
relief to be home again before midday.

Tuesday morning, a call from the kitchen
"Could you get me some milk from the Co-op"
"Oh, and don't forget your mask"
A moderate queue had formed outside the entrance with a
'Do not enter the store until another customer leaves' sign
lots of time for greetings and distanced chatting as
friends and neighbours stood in an orderly line

On arriving home "You've been a long time" was the greeting
Did I have to explain that queueing wasn't fleeting.

Wednesday morning came along with cold and heavy rain
An umbrella and raincoat were dug out in the hall.
"Could you call at the butchers and get some stewing steak"
came a voice from within and the anticipated yell
"Oh and don't forget your mask"
The 'only three people in the shop at any time' sign had
    appeared.
"Go in on your own", "Wait outside" the stern lady boomed
Fed up but out of the rain and inside the shop at last
'One way', 'Keep apart', 'pay by card'! don't forget
an item as there is no going back round again.
Back home I'm met with "You've been a long time"
 but I had my rolled up paper inside my dripping Mac.

Thursday morning dawned bright and sunny,
better weather for the shopping relay.
The "don't forget your mask" call came as I left home.
As if I would. I was soon back with my paper
"You're early today."

A wet Friday morning, Mac and brolly again.
"Can you call at the chemist for my prescription today"
and the expected "Don't forget your mask." Could I??
Who would queue outside or enter the chemist, where
all the sick and ill folk go to collect their medicinal
needs without a mask anyway?
A 'We don't open until 10 AM' sign. Oh no, 20 minutes to wait
The progression of the long slow moving line had
everyone hiding under umbrellas, not much chatting today.
Arriving home wet and annoyed at the long wait I had to
    endure

When the "You've been a long time" was uttered it was
difficult to keep my scathing remarks to myself. For sure.

Saturday dawned warm, bright and sunny but
the annoying call came with the task
"Call at the fruit shop for potatoes.", "Oh, and don't forget
your mask." I could no longer hold my tongue.
"You don't have to remind me every day. I'm not a child."

The usual wait outside the shop but with a
colleague and neighbour to chat to. I didn't mind.
Home for coffee and the "You've been a long time."
"So would you be if you had to stand in line."

Sunday dawns quietly, a lie-in for my wife.
I take her a cup of tea in bed then leave to get my paper.
Almost at the shop I realise I have forgotten my mask.
Only one thing for it. I would have to slip back home
and steal in and out again so as not to be heard.
"You've been very quick"
"Did you forget your mask?"

The Elusive Seal

I lie awake, listening, silence beckoning, the new dawn waiting, time to rise. The birds embark on their lilting morning chorus. I'll not be late, will you be waiting?

Leaving my night-time shelter, clambering down the steep rugged slope to the deserted tide washed beach far below, no signs of life, the smooth unmarked sand stretches far ahead.

Waiting, watching the dancing waves catching the jewelled morning light, patient yet impatient for the marvel you bring. Then you appear, your black silky head breaks the surface, your questioning eyes watching, you twist and turn in your rolling greeting. Responding to my call, darting forward, diving beneath the rippling waves to appear again far ahead. Walking now, you playing your frolicking game in the shallow water, exhilaration rises, my heart beats faster, running now, you keeping pace, listening to my babble all awhile.

The end of the bay is nearing, fishermen with their morning catch, gulls wheeling, shrieking high above. Your bark causes me to turn but my searching eyes catch no sight of you. The gentle waves have claimed you once more.

Homeward I stroll along the quiet sands, hoping, trusting another dawn will bring me the joy of seeing you once more.

Jean Taylor

Happy Days Remembered

As I get nearer to my end of life
I think of times spent as a mother and wife
Of the places we visited here and there
Seeing all life's wonders everywhere

Favourite times sailing on the sea
Enjoying life and being fancy free
Leaning on the rail and feeling no fear
Clutching our champagne or maybe a beer

Looking up at the stars shining bright
Or the sun going down before the night
Watching the dolphins and fish in the ocean
Or listening to the ships engines in motion

Making new friends and visiting new places
Going on outings and meeting new faces
Finally reaching the last port of call
Rocking and rolling and trying not to fall

Getting back home and needing a rest
While storing our thoughts in our memory chest
Thinking ahead to our next holiday
Where shall we go and where shall we stay.

The Bee Garden

We planted a garden for the bees
We did it on our hands and knees

Then spent our days digging up the weeds
And adding the flowers, plants and seeds

Summer arrived and we sat in delight
As we watched the bees flying left and right

Feeding on the nectar and going to their homes
While we hoped to survive with our weary bones

And continue our gardening day after day
Starting up again in April and May.

Stuart Turner

In the Pennines Far Away

Apologies to Thomas Hardy for borrowing a certain style for this poem. I think it suits this tale of two young boys, aged ten and eight years, who climbed Killhope Law (over 2000 feet in the North Pennines). We climbed from Allenheads youth hostel – our first real mountain experience.

When we planned our mountain trip
Following routes upon the map
We checked, and rechecked, made sure
That there would be no mishap
On bog and rocks, the airy slopes
When we dared to climb the mountain
In the Pennines far away.

When we started up that high hill
Its beauty we did not know
The purple was on the heather
And the cotton grass like snow.
As we carefully picked our way
We felt like great explorers
In the Pennines far away.

Could we dreaming schoolboys win
The summit, high and wild
Through rocks and mist and danger
Though our fathers called us 'child'
The time we went adventuring
In the Pennines far away.

When we reached the very top
With wonder in our souls
We felt we'd gained the gates of heaven
And danced wildly round like lapwings
Then stood silent, felt we should
Triumphant with our famous climb
In the Pennines far away.

Who was Mavis?

Name found on a churchyard bench in County Durham. I don't know who Mavis was but wrote a speculative poem about who she could have been.

Perhaps in the prime of life,
or maybe a girl so fair
or hirpling gamely on
along life's narrow way.

Fair or raven black
her hair in ringlets hung,
a smile on ruby lips
and eyes beguiling sung.

I see on that face
all the worries of a life hard won;
a young woman born to caring,
her heart not filled with sun.

She trod the path that now I walk
for solace in her brief
the tears dripped in the breeze
as time slipped by, a thief.

She'd known a special love
but he went off to war,
and fought 'til he fell dead, perhaps
and left his girl, full sore.

He never did return, alas
to his love so brave and strong
he'd died somewhere in Flanders,
where his soul did not belong.

This lady in duty laboured
with parents old and grey
when they died she felt so tired
her loved ones all away.

A few more years she lingered
her cares she put to use,
by helping other friends to live
and often she did muse.

One day she'd had enough
this lady so forlorn
she died in April, just like this
her mind and heartstrings torn.

So now you know of Mavis,
long gone into the past
and how she struggled onward
till peace she found at last.

Nee Mair Coal

A poem in the vernacular. I actually worked with these men for about two years in our local pit, the Victory, Consett. A way of life gone forever.

Nee mair are th' wagons o' th' track
Filled with coal, running forth and back
T' th' face where canny colliers worked
Mid the soond o' drums when it heaved an' jorked

Gone frae th' dark an' dank an' wet
Are th' lads whe, half naked, corsed and sweat
Tee win th' precious black diamond – coal;
Frae th' bowels o' that rustin' evil hole.

Hock an' Tom an' Ripper, too
Th' lads whe filled, an' pulled an' hew
Caked wi' dust an' choked b' fume
I' th' Victory Pit, the pitman's tomb.

Whenivver aa pass th' owld pithead
Aa think o' days ago lang dead,
When fouled air an' dust minglin' i' th' draft
Or th' ghostlike clank o' th' caige an' shaft.

Th' pulleys stand idle, th' belts are still
Nee clankin' pumps, nee tubs t' fill
Nowt but ghosts an' th' divvil dwell
I' that creakin', groanin' undergroond hell.

Aye – gone th' ponies an' th' stables
Stopped th' winnin', nee mair daytals;
It's factories noo an' shops an' roads
'Stead o' pits an' huge coal loads.

Finished, dead, an' ownly memories see
Waat th' Victory Pit once used t' be.

Sexton

A bit of fun really.

Some yards north of St. Crispin's nave
By a greening hawthorn bush,
The sexton plied his ancient trade,
Serenaded by a thrush.

His task today was almost done,
The allotted six by three space
For a yeoman, name of Fry
Who at ninety had run his race.

The parson hovers, brows furrowed
To see the prelins without strife
As befits this important chap,
A leader in village life.

The primmish churchwarden Mrs Ayton
Oversees the flowers around:
'We must make sure in keeping
With his rank of chief horse and hound.'

The widow Prentice was his friend;
They shared fine things and good wine,
But the master's taste went further
'Twas rumoured, for things clandestine.

The sad day came he was interred,
The huntsmen blew on their horns
In one final blast as a tribute,
While those in the know stifled yawns.

At the banqueting hall of 'The Crown'
The proceedings in full swing,
Speeches given and toasts made
To Fry, his coffin and its bling.

Now alcohol flowed and tongues loosened
Made debate turn to Fry's doings,
Voices were raised, some not too kind
Musing on his comings and goings.

At length an imbiber named Pratt
Talked glibly of Fry's evening calls;
Seen slinking off to the widow's
Who lived close by the priory walls.

And how our sexton smiled again -
He knew well the truth of those nights;
While Reggie Fry was thought dallying,
It was *he* who knew widows' delights.

Yes, the villagers thought it was Reg
Who was plying the lass with gold's gleam.
But in fact he only got milksop,
It was the gravedigger getting the cream.

So beware all you detectives,
Who try two and two to make five...
No notice take of rumour rife
It's the sexton 'the dig' who's alive.

Hiatus

Being interested in local history, Romans had to figure somewhere; written I hope with the tension that the Roman occupation always engendered.

The chief sends his peace envoy
Soldiers wait, plumes flying
Eagles shining
Symbols of power.
Empty handed
The envoy returns.
A small boy whimpers.
The air is tense.

Warriors bronzed but cold faced
Build a fort
At river's crossing;
Symbol of power.
And invasion, fires are lit
To dissembling voices
Fear lingers.

Anxious morning
Fear spreads
Soldiers are alert.
Barbarians have crossed Sulwath;
Symbols of power.
Two hours' march away
The seer Lughain
Consults his runes.

Endless Road

I have always been enthralled by the nation of Gypsies and can count a clan called Faa as acquaintances, if not friends. I abhor their plight, which is undeserved. The Romany Gypsies are a fine people.

There's nowhere to rest, nowhere to stay,
You're born to the roving, along the highway.
'Keep moving on' the councils all say.
There's nowhere to rest, and nowhere to stay.

When the frost it's biting, and the snows have all come,
The travelling folk linger, to seek a brief home.
But like Christ in the manger, and nomads of old,
We're shunned by mankind, turned out in the cold.

We can't use the campsites, though no one's around;
Our pleas are ignored, our cries are all drowned.
Our wives they are desperate, the children are numb
But the people are cheerless, the town halls are dumb.

The caravans are leaking, the horses are lame;
Old Aaron is dying - we cry with the shame.
Oh! Why can't we shelter, be safe from the storm,
'Til the old man finds peace, and the new child is born?

Aye! Our life, like a picture just lies in a frame,
Barred in by orders, and scarred by a name.
Though it seems we are bound like the winds for to roam,
Sing 'Gum sha hack' softly boys, 'til we find our home.

The Moon for a Lamp

The twilight was fading from pinnacled edge
As we clambered on downward, on bilberry ledge,
Insects and lizards and things of the night
Scampered and rustled, still hid from our sight.

A new route of merit we'd done on the wall
And thwarted a buttress, so broken and tall.
As we climbed and belayed over gully and scree
The time was forgotten, in exploratory glee.

So downward we pressed as the daylight cut short;
Happy, contented, and filled by our sport,
Gradually nearing the bright silvered tarn,
Glimpsed between snatches of singing and yarn.

Sounds of the dale echoed in the air,
The owl and some bats, and an old brood mare.
Friendly and kind they were, magic to hear
As we paused our descent to listen and peer.

Our feet plodded wearily on corrie and track,
As the sky passed from blues to a deepening black.
With a dusting of stars, all twinkling and winking
It ceased us our songs and set us to thinking.

Young spirits were up, young hearts all aglow,
  In the indigo sky a bright orb was on show.
    We leaped and we strode, eager for camp,
      Using to guide us the moon for a lamp.

We'd washed and we'd supped and relaxed our limbs,
nd yammered or sprawled and indulged in our whims,
Then later our guide light from cloud banks did peep,
nd of mountain and moonlight we dreamt in our sleep.

A King's Forest

Invaders passed this way
but used only
its heights as passing
watch towers, fearing
barbarians
to the north.
Beyond a high
and mighty barrier
a dynasty died
here too, then
others followed
Fierce, conquering
settling, leaving
place names.

The land was tamed
A place of hunting
and sport
fit for
a king.
The wood pig,
killer of men
lived here
and deer, bound
for a king's table
and his larders.

Yet wild, sparse
ever threatening
things followed,
more modern.
Blue faced minions
dug holes in the
moorland, to extract
rocks that glinted
in sunlight
Polluting streams
leaving scars.

At its southern end
unholy beings stalked
the night, renowned
for blood letting
Terror prevailed nearby.
Holy men from
over the western sea
as if in opposition
built a place of worship.
The stream lets and
land flourished
curlew, buzzard and
raptors flew, high
over empty hills.

Wild and silent
with only
whispering
grasses and rolling
seas of mauve in sight.
The odd human, a few
hawks and indigenous
ghosts remain, guardians
of an ancient wasteland –
A king's forest.

Off to Sea Once More

*Written following a holiday in northwest Scotland
some years ago on a rather windblown, grey evening.
The atmosphere was quite amazing.*

While we stood shivering on the point
The boats put out once more,
Beating northward through the night,
Shunned from the windbound shore.

The gulls in squadrons cried 'Farewell!
We'll wait for your return!'
But riding lights were blotted out,
The squall had closed again.

Earth and sea and sky are one
Fused in a forlorn grey
The north wind moaned, and shattered ruins
Of a croft, lay – rank and bare.

The boats had gone, the zenith black
Was riven with angry storms,
We scurried home through bog and rock
Two draggled, thoughtful forms.

The water slopped, the water fell
An owl betrayed the mood
A way of life went on, unseen
About us, darkness stood.

Wilderness Flowers

I love the flowers of the high North Pennines of which the spring gentian is the prize specimen at The Heap in Teesdale. Other lesser specimens do exist elsewhere in our hills; the location is known only to myself.

Seed saved
Brought up by bird beak
And soughing wind
Cocooned, protected
Flower, it took me
Four years to flourish
Now I'm here
Always.

The Shilling Volunteer

'Dulce et decorum est pro patria mori.' A personal poem, written for my great-great uncle who served and died at nineteen years old in World War One. He was one of two young family members who travelled to Flanders only to die in the mud, stench and barbarism of trench warfare.

When I felt the urgent call
To keep my country free,
Little did I think just then
Such carnage would I see.

The bodies stiff and bloody,
The fields so full of gore;
Whole battalions bleeding
Like the slaughter days of yore.

An enemy without mercy
Who killed for killing's sake,
And me, a shilling volunteer
Saw swift my conscience wake.

I fought through hell
At Paschendale and Ypres
In stinking trenches, stunned
Saw others slumped into eternal sleep.

I fought with others
Till I fell, exhausted
From wounds and clinging mud
And cried at the victory, just as a baby would.

The colonel, he promoted me
To a sergeant's rank I was made:
'The others are out of it, dead,' he croaked.
'Do it for your country's sake.'

As I passed over I thought
How miraculously sweet a thing;
I had died for king and country
Then I heard the old bells ring.

In Flanders mud I lie
Under the stinking filth and clay
A shilling volunteer –
Who missed peace by one day.

On a monument in my village
In two lines engraved quite clear:
'To the memory of Cecil Moody,
A shilling volunteer.'

Holy Island

*A short poem to reflect a day's travel
to the famous island and shrine to the
'Geordie saint' St. Cuthbert.*

Tidal road crossed
Dreaming castle and
Venerable relics

Boats on shore
Land lubbers
Sun on seaweed

Pink thrift and
Discarded nets
Lobster pots around
Waiting.

Evening from Talkin Fell

The silver Solway gleams afar,
Contented sounds from the plain below.
The softening peace, the evening star
Held fast amidst the sunset glow.

Dream

It was a day for dreaming,
when all the sunbeams danced;
I fell in a deep deep slumber
and lay there quite entranced.
From the shadows of the mind,
where the fleeting images play
I journeyed on the Silk Road,
half a world away.

I saw again the merchants
in those caravans of old
With their silks and spices from the East,
more precious things than gold.
With a nutmeg-brown skinned trader
in a camp on a pass so high,
We talked of the deeds of Kubla Khan
under a fabled saffron sky.

We spoke of dragons and of kings,
and of dynasties so old
There were ancient kingdoms crumbling
as our dear Christ's life was told.
I heard of battles and unicorns,
of the works of poets afar
Gathered flowers like our own harebells,
under the evening star.

I felt so privileged, honoured
As my experience turned to day
Where I'd journeyed on the Silk Road
Half a world away.

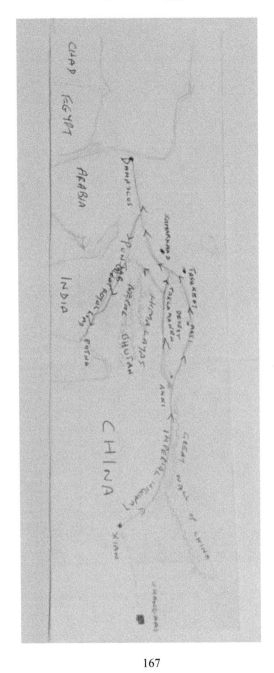

Thank you for buying this Anthology

Now here is some space for you to add some poems of your own

Poetry Anthology No.3

Lightning Source UK Ltd.
Milton Keynes UK
UKHW012219220321
380796UK00001B/48

9 781838 017736